AUSTRALIA

Published by Brolga Publishing Pty Ltd
ABN 46 063 962 443
PO Box 12544
A'Beckett St
Melbourne, VIC, 8006
Australia

email: markzocchi@brolgapublishing.com.au

National Library of Australia Cataloguing-in-Publication data

Creator:	Peters, Susan Margaret, author.
Title:	Australia / Susan Peters.
ISBN:	9781922175656 (hardback)
Subjects:	Australia--Description and travel--Pictorial works.
	Australia--Pictorial works.
Dewey Number:	919.400222

Printed in China
Photography & Cover images by Susan Peters
Darwin photography by Rosi Griffin
Brisbane, Uluru and Perth stock photos from Shutterstock.com
Design & Typesetting by Brolga Publishing & Susan Peters

BE PUBLISHED

Publish through a successful publisher. National distribution, Macmillan & International distribution to the United Kingdom, North America. Sales Representation to South East Asia
Email: markzocchi@brolgapublishing.com.au

AUSTRALIA

Photography by Susan Peters

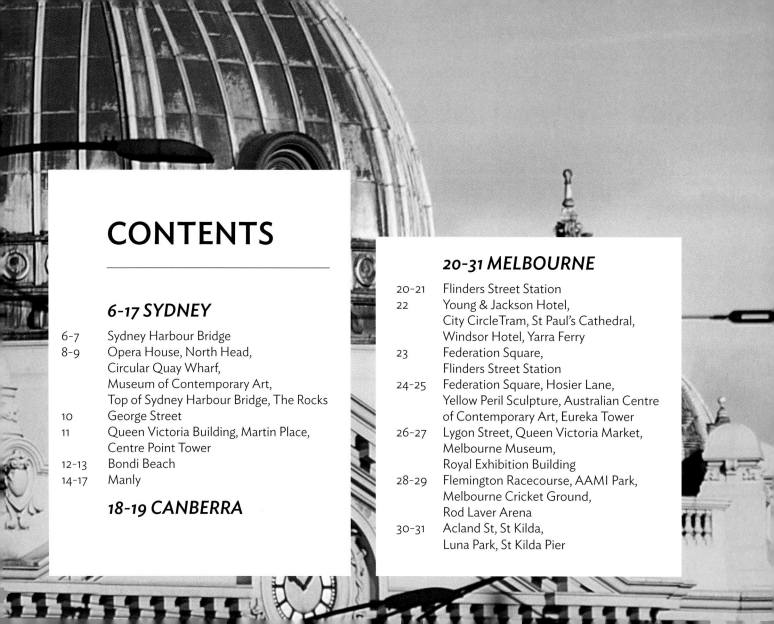

CONTENTS

YOU IMAGINE
WHAT YOU DESIRE

MCARe

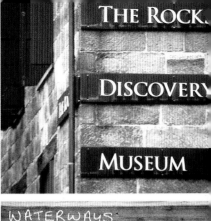

THE ROCK.

DISCOVERY

MUSEUM

METCALF

Circular
Quay

WATERWAYS
300 x 256 - 9·2 M   o/n 488

WATERWAYS
300' x 300 - 9·2 M   o/n 488

SYDNEY

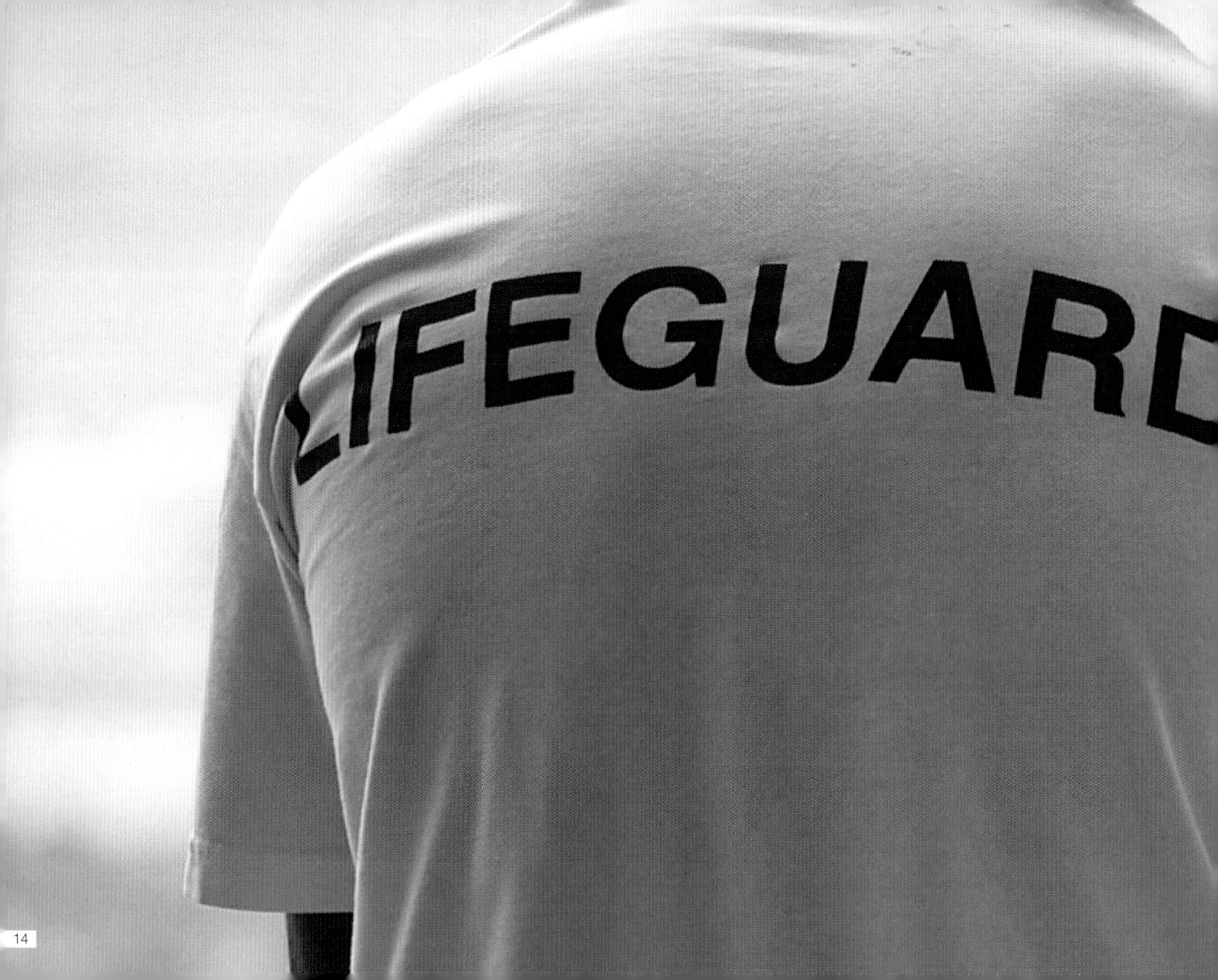
LIFEGUARD

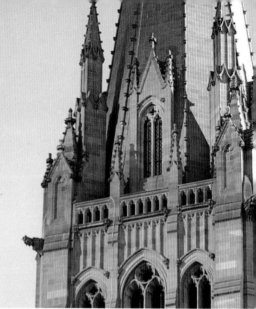

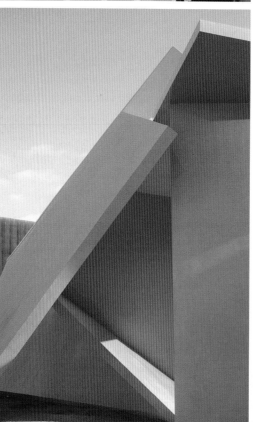

MELBOURNE MUSEUM

Readings

FLEMINGTON

Canecutter's Cottage

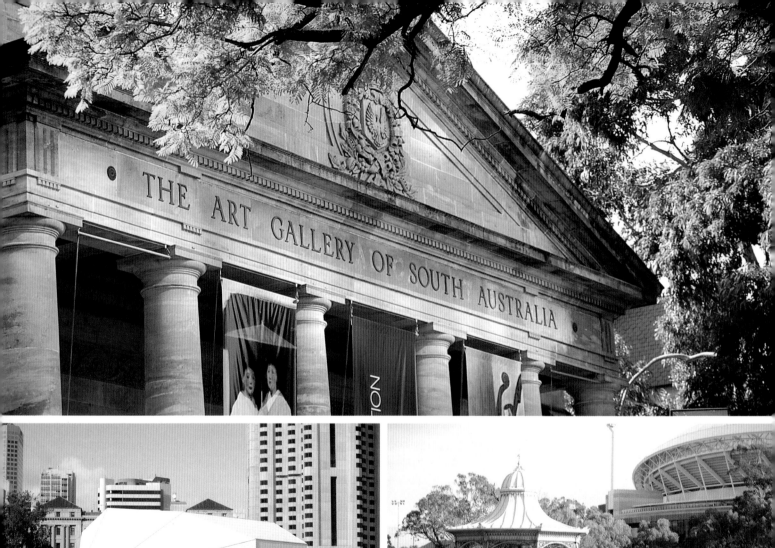

ADELAIDE
ARCADE

CHAPPELL STAND

310 ↑

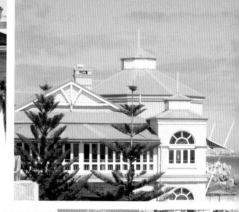

Susan Peters is a Visual and Fine Arts graduate of Melbourne's Swinburne and Monash universities.

Her passion for contemporary art extends to photography, painting, sculpure, print-media, video and installation work.

She has most recently been applying her skills at a leading private school delivering the art program in their Reggio Emilia inspired Early Learning Centre.

Susan's commissioned and private photography reflects her artistic view of the world.

Visit her website at
susanpetersshadowpony.com

AUSTRALIA
Susan Peters

ISBN 9781922175656   Qty

RRP   AU$14.99   .....

Postage within Australia   AU$5.00   .....

TOTAL* $_____

* All prices include GST

Name:..

Address:..

....

Phone:..

Email:..

Payment: q Money Order q Cheque q MasterCard q Visa

Cardholders Name:..

Credit Card Number:...

Signature:...

Expiry Date:..

Allow 7 days for delivery.

Payment to: Marzocco Consultancy (ABN 14 067 257 390)
PO Box 12544
A'Beckett Street, Melbourne, 8006
Victoria, Australia
admin@brolgapublishing.com.au